Enlarging the Union

THE INTERGOVERNMENTAL CONFERENCE OF THE EUROPEAN UNION
1996

Federal Trust Papers Number Five

THE FEDERAL TRUST

The Federal Trust was founded in 1945 to study the future of democratic unity between states and peoples. The principal focus of its work has been the European Union and the United Kingdom's role within it.

The Federal Trust conducts enquiries, promotes seminars and conferences and publishes on a wide range of contemporary issues — most recently (apart from the IGC) on pensions reform and on the European information society. Its current work programme includes a study of public-private partnerships in the European Union.

The Trust has also established a major European education programme for sixth forms, universities and young leaders. It is involved in several projects to enhance the European dimension in the curriculum.

The Federal Trust is the UK member of TEPSA (the Trans-European Policy Studies Association).

PUBLISHED BY THE FEDERAL TRUST
11 TUFTON STREET
LONDON SW1P 3QB

© FEDERAL TRUST FOR EDUCATION AND RESEARCH, FEBRUARY 1996

ISBN 0 90157354 X
ISSN 1357 3314

Federal Trust Round Table

The Federal Trust Round Table was established to discuss in depth the issues raised by the 1996 Intergovernmental Conference of the European Union, to monitor the processes of its preparation, negotiation and ratification, and, later, to assess its outcome.

The following **Federal Trust Papers** were published in 1995:

No. 1	*State of the Union*	February
No. 2	*Towards the Single Currency*	May
No. 3	*Building the Union: reform of the institutions*	
		June
No. 4	*Security of the Union*	October

Besides *Enlarging the Union*, more **Federal Trust Papers** are planned for 1996 and, depending on the progress of the IGC, beyond. The next, No. 6, *Justice and Fair Play*, will appear in April.

The Round Table is chaired by Lord Jenkins of Hillhead, President of the European Commission 1977-81; the rapporteur is John Pinder, Chairman of the Federal Trust; the secretary is Andrew Duff, Director of the Trust, to whom any written comments should be addressed.

The members of the Round Table, shown on the following page, serve in an independent capacity and do not represent their organisations. They do not necessarily concur with all the opinions expressed in this **Federal Trust Paper**, but they support its general thrust and welcome it as a contribution to the debate about the future of the Union.

The Federal Trust is an independent charity and, as such, holds no political view of its own.

Members of the Federal Trust Round Table

Glossary

CAP	Common Agricultural Policy
CFSP	Common Foreign and Security Policy
CIS	Commonwealth of Independent States
Comecon	Council for Mutual Economic Assistance
Ecu	European Currency Unit
EEA	European Economic Area
EFTA	European Free Trade Area
EMU	Economic and Monetary Union
EU	European Union
ERM	Exchange Rate Mechanism
GATT	Global Agreement on Tariff and Trade
GDP	Gross Domestic Product
IGC	Intergovernmental Conference
Nato	North Atlantic Treaty Organisation
OECD	Organisation for Economic Cooperation and Development
Phare	Pologne et Hongrie: Aide à la Restructuration Economique: since 1992 the programme has covered all countries of Central and Eastern Europe
WEU	Western European Union
Visegrad	Trilateral agreement between Poland, Czechoslovakia and Hungary signed in February 1991

Enlarging the Union [1]

> 'Only a fool who has learned nothing from the millennia of European history can believe that tranquillity, peace and prosperity can flourish for ever in one part of Europe, without regard for what is happening in the other parts'.
>
> VACLAV HAVEL
> *European Parliament, March 1994*

The dramatic events of 1989, the collapse of the Communist system in Eastern Europe, followed soon after by the fragmentation of the Soviet Union itself, presented Europe with three historic opportunities: to unify Germany, to end the division of Europe, and to make a decisive contribution to a new world order.

Thanks to Chancellor Kohl and President Gorbachev, the first opportunity was seized with unexpected rapidity: Germany was unified in 1990. This meant simultaneous enlargement of the territory of the European Community, by the adhesion of the five Eastern Länder, the former German Democratic Republic, and their 17 million inhabitants to the Federal Republic.

The second prospect opened up in 1989 was the opportunity to heal the half-century old division of Europe by embedding unified Germany into an enlarged and more closely integrated European Union (EU). The Maastricht Treaty, signed in 1991 and ratified by late 1993, was an effort to make progress in the direction of European Union. Enlargement of the Union to admit former Communist states was agreed in principle by the European Council in June 1993, holding out the prospect of extending to Central and Eastern Europe the benefits of integration, as well as further enhancing the stability and prosperity of Western Europe.

The third opportunity, to create a new world order in place of the Cold War division, lies largely outside the scope of this Paper. But the European Union's ability to play a crucial role in the reform of the United Nations and the building of more effective global security will be measured against its contribution to pan-European prosperity, security and stability. If it fails in Europe, it cannot expect to succeed elsewhere.

Success in widening the Union to incorporate the forgotten half of Europe should bring great benefits; failure in the attempt would be a great blow to the credibility of the Union, risking a reversion to the dangerous system of competing national states of the 1920s and 1930s, inevitably a dominant role for Germany certainly in Central Europe and probably in Western Europe, and the danger of renewed intra-European conflicts. The European Union, therefore, has an overriding responsibility to ensure pan-European stability and security; enlargement is a vital challenge: there is no alternative.

Enlargement and the 1996 IGC

Against this background of historic opportunity, the original agenda of the 1996 Intergovernmental Conference (IGC) could appear parochial.[2] The IGC was set up in order to improve the effectiveness of the institutions of the Union. Enlargement was a second thought, but a sound one — extraneous to the original purpose of the 1996 IGC, but recognised as having a potentially crucial influence on the outcome. Arguably, indeed, enlarging the Union has become the major strategic imperative driving the IGC. Without a successful IGC it will be difficult and risky to enlarge the Union; without the pressure of enlargement it will hardly be possible the make the IGC succeed.

The European Council at Copenhagen in June 1993 agreed that:

> 'the associated countries in central and eastern Europe that so desire shall become members of the European Union. Accession will take place as soon as an associated country is able to assume the obligations of membership by satisfying the economic and political conditions required.'[3]

These conditions were:

- stability of institutions guaranteeing democracy, the rule of law, human rights and respect for and the protection of minorities;
- the existence of a functioning market economy as well as the capacity to cope with competitive pressure and market forces within the Union;
- ability to take on the obligations of membership including adherence to the aims of political, economic and monetary union.

The European Union has taken practical steps to assist potential applicants to fulfil these conditions in various bilateral 'Europe Agreements', that involve institutional dialogue, trade agreements, and financial and technical assistance. We discuss their value below, on page 29.

Enlargement, moreover, has become a key factor in the current dynamics of European integration, being widely supported even by governments and public opinion which are sceptical about other proposed changes in institutions or policies. While most supporters of enlargement are genuine and well-intentioned, some are superficial and even simplistic. And there are a few who are disingenuous in their expressions of support for enlargement — hoping that a rapid expansion of the Union will enfeeble its supranational institutions and put federalism in retreat.

Enlargement will certainly have a dramatic effect on the Union. The eventual accession of all the actual and prospective applicants would raise the Union's population by over 100 million to about 475 million. Enlargement will also have a decisive influence on several decisions which have to be taken soon after the end of the IGC — on reforms to Union policies, especially for agriculture and the structural funds, on the size and shape of the EU budget, and on the future of the Western European Union (WEU).

In this Paper we ask whether there is a realistic basis for the accession of the more likely candidates by the early years of the next century. First we turn to the terms and conditions that may be attached by the Union to the new members.

Past and future enlargements

From six members at the outset, the EU expanded to nine in 1973, ten in 1981, twelve in 1986 and fifteen in 1995. Applications have been received, or are expected imminently, from a further thirteen states: Poland, the Czech Republic, Slovakia, Hungary, Slovenia, Romania, Bulgaria, Estonia, Latvia, Lithuania, Cyprus, Malta and Turkey. The candidacy of five further states, Croatia, Bosnia-Herzegovina, Serbia-Montenegro, Macedonia and Albania, has been indefinitely delayed by the Balkan War, although Albania and Macedonia have been admitted to the Council of Europe, a significant staging post to European integration. Further candidates could emerge eventually from the Commonwealth of Independent States (CIS) — Moldova and Ukraine are already in the Council of Europe — though the question of further EU enlargement in that area is too uncertain to require much discussion at present. The futures of the Russian Federation and Belarus are unpredictable, but the possibility that stability will only be secured by the installation of a military or a fiercely nationalistic government in Moscow cannot be discounted. In this case, Russia's membership of the Council of Europe is likely to remain controversial.

To complete the jigsaw, applications to join the EU might one day be forthcoming from Iceland, Norway (again); and even Switzerland which, with Liechtenstein, has already applied, may be able to take the plunge.

The prospective enlargement is not only much larger than any of the previous accretions of additional states to the original Six; it is also qualitatively different, since it involves applicants that languished under Communist systems during the forty years when Western Europe made rapid progress in economic development and integration. This enlargement will not be easy; hence the three conditions stipulated by the Copenhagen European Council.

The political conditions are onerous.[4] The applicants will have to convince the existing member states and the European Parliament that their judiciaries are independent and the rule of law supreme, that elections are properly conducted and fully pluralistic, that their parliaments have real power, that local government has some autonomy from central government, that the rights of individual citizens and private associations are affirmed in the constitution, that ethnic and linguistic minorities are protected in law and respected in practice, that their press and media are free to speak the truth, and that their military are under political control. As its performance over the ratification of Turkey's customs union agreement attested, the European Parliament will be tempted to block enlargement unless an absolute majority of its Members are satisfied on all these issues. Under the Phare and other programmes, the applicant states are receiving much technical assistance and political know-how from the EU; most of the applicants have made considerable progress towards these indicators of political convergence — although Romania, Bulgaria, Slovakia and the Baltic States are still some distance from meeting some of the criteria.

The economic conditions are also demanding, since they require completing an unprecedented transition from centrally-directed to market economy. The applicants are still battling with the legacy of socialist economic management, with a distended public sector, inadequate banking and other financial institutions, a paucity of entrepreneurs and trained managers, and an overweening, officious and in many cases corrupt bureaucracy. They have to complete a massive reform of property law, corporate governance, financial discipline and tax legislation, as well as the privatisation of much of their still large public sector and restrictions on state aids, before they can begin to conform to EU single market regulations and face EU competition in their own markets. They must also carry through painful macro-economic stabilisation programmes.

The capacity of applicants both to accept and to fully understand the dynamic obligations of membership will have to be proven beyond reasonable doubt. The threshold of the acquis communautaire has been progressively raised since 1952. The original Six formed a coal and steel community and then a customs union; the first enlargement in 1973 required the UK, Denmark and Ireland to join a common market, including common agricultural and fisheries policies; Spain and Portugal joined in 1986 as the EC was committing itself to the single market; in 1995 Austria, Finland and Sweden had to embrace at once the Treaty on European Union, including Economic and Monetary Union (EMU). The magnitude of the adjustments to be made by new members has been raised at every step: the 1996 IGC and the imminent transition to Stage Three of EMU will serve to do so again.

Given their starting point, another kind of threshold for the Central and East Europeans, that of relative prosperity, is steep. The GDP per capita of all the applicants is currently below half the EU average. But the gap in real income levels for the more advanced Central Europeans compares none too badly with that of the poorer Western member states at the time of their accession, all of whom had GDPs of 55% or less of the EC average.

GDP PER CAPITA AS PERCENTAGE OF EU AVERAGE [5]		
EU members at accession	*New Applicants in 1993*	
Ireland (1973) 53	Slovenia	50
Greece (1981) 44	Czech Republic	42
Spain (1986) 55	Estonia	38
Portugal (1986) 27	Hungary	36
	Slovakia	34
	Bulgaria	33
	Poland	32
	Latvia	29
	Lithuania	18
	Romania	16

These comparisons are provided only as broad indicators and should not be interpreted as accurate statistics on the basis of which narrow policy conclusions can be drawn.[6] Note also that the table compares EU members in the year of accession with the applicants in 1993: by the time the latter accede their faster rates of growth should have closed some of the gap.

Under the terms of the Treaty, the accession of any new European state has to be agreed by the Union unanimously, ratified with due constitutional procedures — parliamentary or referendum, or both — in each member state, and also by the European Parliament, acting by absolute majority.[7] Accession must also be ratified by the applicant states, a feat not achieved by Norway in 1972 and 1994 — nor de facto by Switzerland when it lost a referendum on membership of the European Economic Area in December 1992. There are many reasons why such agreement and ratification could be withheld, ranging from a judgement that the applicant had failed to meet the dual test of liberal democracy and market economy, hostility to new competition and higher EU spending, to negative public opinion. Enlargement, clearly, can never be taken for granted. Since the consequences of rejection would be so serious for the applicants, and damaging to the EU itself, the process leading to accession needs to be prepared carefully, with efforts on both sides to ensure a successful outcome.

Disappointment with failure would be intense. Public opinion in Central and Eastern Europe is overwhelmingly in favour of EU membership — ranging from over 90% in Slovenia to 70% in European Russia.[8] This sentiment is also reflected in commerce and industry: in a recent survey the vast majority of companies indicated that further European integration was very important to themselves and to their competitors.[9] Public opinion in the EU is less exuberant about the prospect of eastern enlargement but still sympathetic: ranging from 55% in favour of Hungarian accession to 45% for Romania.[10]

Who should join, and when?

The enlargement question overwhelmingly concerns Central Europe, which separates the European Union from the former Soviet Union. Poland, the Czech Republic, Slovakia, Hungary and Slovenia border on Germany or Austria and are capable of close industrial integration with the existing members. Their accession is of great political and economic significance and high priority. After traumatic declines in GDP following the collapse of the Soviet market and disruption associated with the transition to market economies, by the end of 1995 these countries were recovering well and are forecast to enjoy strong economic growth in the mid-1990s. We consider each case here, followed by that of the three Baltic states, the two East European neighbours, Romania and Bulgaria, and, finally, the three Mediterranean candidates.

Poland is by far the largest applicant with 39 million people, and occupies a vital strategic location. Politically it has had a plethora of political parties and numerous changes of government; reformed Communists have gradually made their return to government since 1994.

Poland's economic transition programme has however brought remarkably good results at the cost of considerable hardship. Its growth was around 5 or 6% per annum during 1994 and 1995.

The *Czech Republic*, with just over ten million people, is capable of especially close integration with the German and Austrian economies, since its industrial centres, well advanced in the 1930s even if stagnant during the Communist era, are geographically highly accessible. Under a popular president, Havel, and a strong prime minister, Klaus, the Czechs have enjoyed political stability and made steady progress in democratisation, economic stabilisation and privatisation. By 1995 70% of the economy was in private ownership, inflation was under control, and growth was accelerating from 3% in 1994 to a forecast 5% in 1996. Czech economic success was recognised by its acceptance as the first former Communist member of the Organisation for Economic Cooperation and Development (OECD) in 1995.

With 5.3 million people, *Slovakia* has special problems since its break-away from the Czech Republic in 1993. Assertive nationalistic politics (prime minister Meciar governs with the support of two more extreme nationalist parties) are heightened by the problem of a Hungarian minority amounting to more than 10% of the population. Slovakia's uncompetitive heavy industries leave the new republic with a massive problem of reconstruction. But privatisation appears to be advancing, with 60% of the economy in at least nominal private ownership by 1995; inflation is under control, and GDP is growing at around 4 - 5%.

In the first years after Communism, *Hungary*, with over ten million people, attracted the lion's share of foreign direct investments in Central and Eastern Europe — $6.9 bn out of a regional total of $17.7 bn in 1989-94, compared

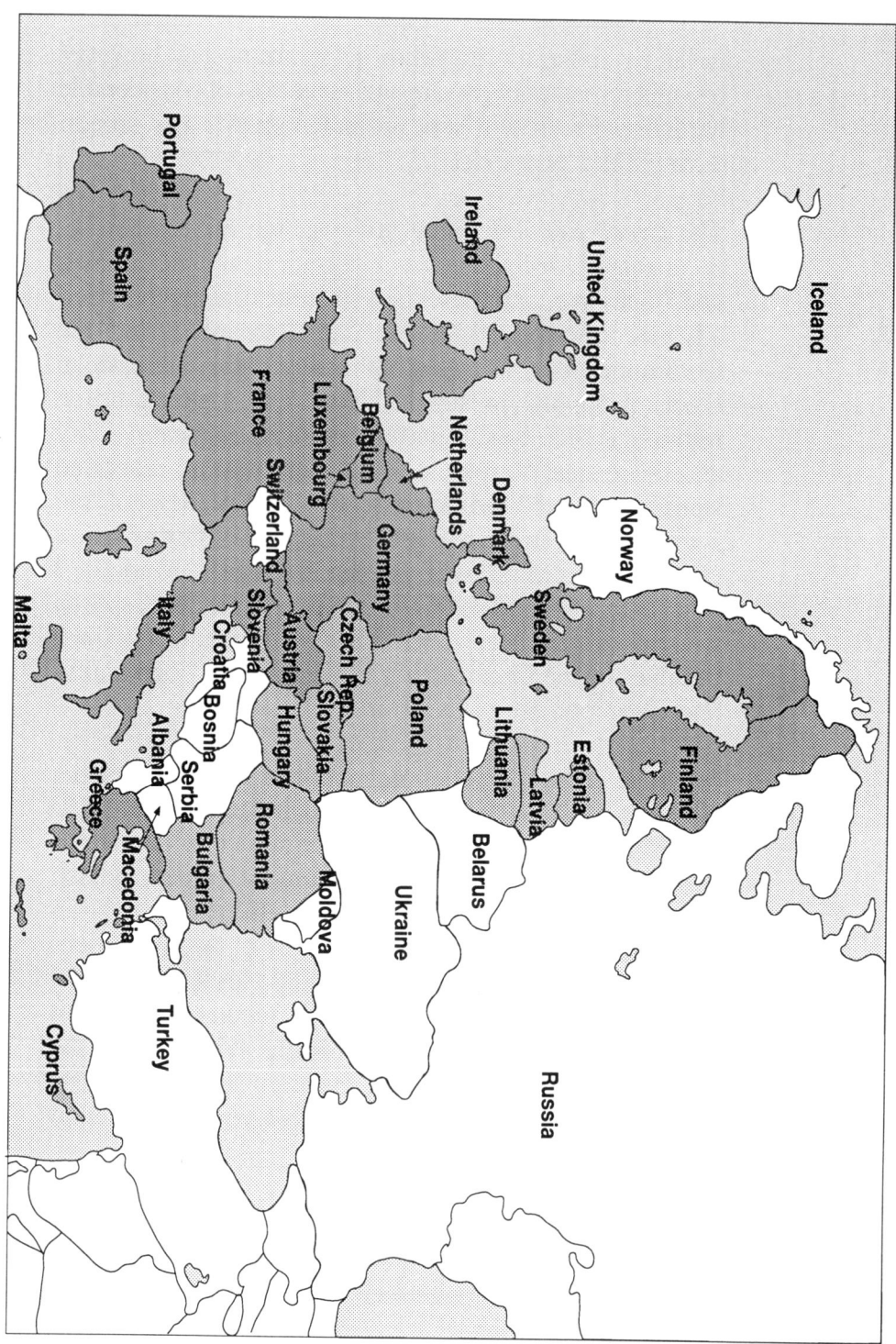

to $3 bn for the Czech Republic and only $1.5 bn for Poland. Of all the countries of the Soviet bloc, Hungary had the longest apprenticeship in moving towards the market economy. Nevertheless, a large external debt overhang has created special difficulties for Hungarian macroeconomic policy, and government management has been shaky. During 1995 budget and payments deficits have been brought under control, but at the cost of reducing GDP growth to less than 1%. Large ethnic Hungarian minorities in Slovakia, Romania and Serbia create problems in relations with these neighbouring states, but so far these have been handled with restraint. The former Communists returned to power in the 1994 elections, under prime minister Horn, but in coalition with the Free Democrats (Liberals), and have demonstrated democratic responsibility. Hungary was the first ex-Communist country to apply for EU membership, in April 1994.

Slovenia escaped virtually unscathed in its short war of independence from Yugoslavia in 1991, and has the most highly developed and best managed economy among the former Yugoslav republics. Growth has been about 5 - 6% since 1994, and GDP per capita is ahead of all the other applicant states. Slovenia's politics are stable and democratic. Disputes with Italy over the restitution of property to former inhabitants seem likely to be resolved. Slovenia is thus a credible candidate, and is likely to be in the first group of applicants to gain accession. Slovenia, with only two million people (and like the Baltic states) falls into a category of small states which will present the EU with specific institutional problems.

In the Baltic, *Lithuania* (3.7 million), *Latvia* (2.7 million) and *Estonia* (1.5 million), despite being former Soviet republics, have been able to assert their independence by keeping out of the CIS. Problematic relations with Russia, however, remain both an impetus for seeking EU membership and a reason for caution on the EU side. The main issue is the treatment of the substantial Russian ethnic minorities in Estonia and Latvia. Language conditions for voters, understandable as these nations seek to reassert their independent statehood, discriminate against Russian-speaking citizens, and are inconsistent with Western standards of civil rights. Moreover, formidable economic problems must be overcome before the Baltic trio, devastated by the break-up of the Soviet Union, are capable of facing up to competition. Estonia is the most advanced in GDP per capita and in economic transition, with 6% annual growth in recent years, and it has close links with the Nordic countries.

Romania, with nearly 23 million people, is almost as large as the Czech Republic, Hungary and Slovakia together, but less advanced industrially, and more distant from the current borders of the European Union. There are serious concerns about the depth of its political revolution, and the existence of the large Hungarian minority in Transylvania has triggered a strong nationalist reaction. The large agricultural sector threatens great costs for the EU budget, and 60% of the economy is still in the public sector. Since 1994, however, GDP is growing at a rate of 4 - 5%, and a quickening of reform in Romania should at no time be excluded.[11]

Bulgaria, with 8.4 million people, is making a slow transition to a market economy and private ownership, with even nominal privatisation leaving more than half the economy still in public ownership. Growth resumed a modest rate of 3% per annum by 1995.

Turkey, with over 60 million people and a high rate of population growth, has a vital strategic location between South-East Europe, the Middle East and the CIS. It has an EC association agreement dating back to 1963, and since January 1996 a customs union with the Union. Turkey's economic growth and industrial development have been impressive, though accompanied by political instability and high inflation. Its application for full membership dates back to 1986, but has not progressed because of concerns about its democratic credentials and human rights record — especially with regard to the treatment of the Kurdish minority. There are also fears about the economic consequences of Turkish accession in terms of trade, the budget and the labour market, an uneasy awareness of the strength of Islamic fundamentalism, and a wide scepticism about its European identity. Nevertheless, the customs union, if it endures, will bring about a large and rapid expansion of exports to the EU and investment from it. If structural reform continues, Turkey's transformation could be dramatic.[12]

Malta and Cyprus applied to join the EU in 1990. In March 1995 the Council promised that negotiations would commence within six months of the end of the IGC; neither, however, is likely to enter before the first wave of Central Europeans.

As long as northern *Cyprus* remains under Turkish control, however, the Union's relations with Turkey will be strained. The Commission's Opinion on the Cyprus application, delivered in 1993, stated that integration of Cyprus into the Community will depend on a 'peaceful, balanced and lasting settlement' of the conflict between the country's two communities.[13] Competition with other Mediterranean agricultural and low-tech industrial producers presents some problems, though Cyprus is small enough for these to be manageable. But Cyprus, with 0.7 million people, raises the question of how EU institutions can cope with micro-states, and the Commission has rightly requested that the 1996 IGC should address this problem.

Malta, with only 350,000 people, poses that same institutional problem even more acutely. Maltese accession, too, would bring the territory of the Union much closer to troubled and unstable North Africa, notably Libya, raising familiar issues about immigration and security.

Faced with the diversity of applicant states and the scale of the problems they represent to the Union, it is inevitable that there is as yet no consensus among existing member states about which or how many applicants should be admitted, or when. Some applicants are obviously more readily absorbed than others, and various suggestions have been made for differentiating between them — for example, that Slovenia could be admitted soon; that Poland is a priority; that negotiations should open with all the original 'Visegrad Four' together (or that Slovakia should be left behind); that Romania and Bulgaria will not be ready for many years; that the Baltic States cannot be considered before relations with Russia have been clarified.

Giving priority to some applicants risks sending negative signals to others, and could exacerbate certain differences among them — for instance, the position of the Hungarian minority in Romania. This has led to suggestions that accession negotiations should open with all ten Central and East European countries on the same date, leaving different rates of progress in resolving problems to determine the order of accession. This proposal was discussed by the European Council in Madrid in December 1995, where the technical problem arose of the Commission's limited capacity to issue Opinions on so many applications, and of the Council's capacity to conduct so many negotiations at once.[14] The problem is not resolved, and the danger remains that the accession negotiations will drag on too long and demotivation or demoralisation will set in on either side. The most serious objection to the idea of one large-scale simultaneous negotiation, however, is the very wide difference in levels of social, economic and political development between the core Central European states and the more peripheral Eastern ones. Assuming that the discrimination we suggest here is reflected in the timetable for accession, the Union should prepare itself to be joined by only four or five new member states from Central Europe by the end of the century — Poland, the Czech Republic, Hungary, Slovenia and, one may hope, Slovakia — but to assume gradual expansion thereafter to possibly 32 member states within two decades.

Fifteen attitudes to enlargement

Since the accession of each new member has to be agreed by each existing member state, it is important to realise that the general consensus among the Fifteen on the principle of enlargement hides wide differences about the scope and timing of specific enlargements, and on what policy and institutional reforms should be made by the Union to accommodate the new members. These disagreements were aired by the Group of Reflection on the IGC, where the prospect of enlargement served to sharpen the debate about 'flexibility', or differentiated integration within the existing Union. But, because of the British fixation on minimising the scale and significance of the IGC, the Reflection Group carefully avoided making any judgement about the impact of enlargement on common policies or resources.[15]

> *Germany* has been most enthusiastic about eastern enlargement, having most to gain economically from exploiting a wider European single market, and the greatest interest in 'projecting security' eastwards. Although unification was handled in ways that created great strains in Germany itself and for Germany's EU partners, the worst effects are now past, and German leadership of the movement towards a wider and deeper Union can again be effective. But three major difficulties could yet inhibit decisive German leadership towards enlarging the Union while at the same time endowing it at the IGC with the powers to make and keep it effective.

First, the Bundesbank and the public seem to be sceptical about the capacity of a new single currency to match the stability and strength of the Deutschmark. Secondly, the insistence of the Constitutional Court and the Bundestag that implementation of Maastricht, including the single currency, should be accompanied by democratic reform, and especially an enhanced role for the EP, is not matched by some other states, which insist also on keeping the second and third pillars intergovernmental. Thirdly, Germany is likely to have difficulty in welcoming without equivocation accession treaties that imply higher net contributions to the EU budget. This suggests that another round of tough negotiations will have to begin in parallel with the IGC on the 'financial perspective' of the EU budget after 1998 — with the UK rebate as a possible German target.

The *Benelux* countries share much of the German approach; *Denmark* has reservations about the deepening federal character of the Union, but will be broadly supportive.

France, on the other hand, has been less enthusiastic than Germany about eastern enlargement, though cultural links with Romania could be important in determining the outcome of that candidacy. The commitment to monetary union has survived the exchange rate and domestic industrial crises of 1995 and seems to remain firm despite its costs in terms of high real interest rates and high unemployment. Furthermore, France is more enthusiastic about building within Nato an effective European pillar for defence cooperation, and, given its long-standing and close alliance with Germany, is now prepared to accept at least some of the main institutional changes that enlargement will necessitate. In December 1995 President Chirac agreed with Chancellor Kohl that it was 'indispensable to give the Union more efficient institutions'.[16] However, reforms to the Common Agricultural Policy (CAP), intended to reduce the costs of applying it to Central Europe, will face strong opposition from French agricultural lobbies.

The *United Kingdom* remains after 23 years of membership a problematic member of the Union. The present government is sceptical about EMU, strongly attached to the intergovernmental approach to Common Foreign and Security Policy, and largely hostile to developing Cooperation in Justice and Home Affairs. It supports enlargement as a means of enhancing European security, but is perceived as being motivated by an assumption that enlargement could mean dilution, preventing further deepening of the EU, and keeping it as little more than a single market organisation. The UK will be keen to reform the institutions of an enlarged EU to reduce the powers of small states. However, political developments within the UK may bring a change of European policy.

Italy favours enlargement and a federal European Union. But the current domestic political confusion and continuing economic problems are major inhibitions on Italy playing a strong role. Furthermore, the southern members are potentially the most reluctant to accept eastern enlargement, as their industries fear intensified competition. *Spain*, *Portugal*, *Greece*, and *Ireland* currently benefit most from EU budget transfers, and on the accession of Austria, Finland and Sweden in 1995 were granted further benefits from the structural funds and the new Cohesion Fund. The richer member states will resist attempts to repeat this kind of trade-off in order to implement eastern enlargement. It is difficult to see how the new enlargement can take place without some parts of the existing EU, including some British regions, being 'graduated' from receipt of EU finance. Spain is particularly agitated on this point.

Among the three newest member states, *Austria* brings a strong interest in the accession to the Union of the former territories of the Habsburg Dual Monarchy in Poland, the Czech Republic, Slovakia, Hungary and Slovenia. *Finland* and *Sweden* have historical and cultural links, as well as current economic interests, in the Baltic States, as well as a strong security interest in helping to keep them independent from Russia and a firm resolve to bring them into the Union.

With such differentiated interests and attitudes towards enlargement and its implications for the balance of policies, the 1993 agreement in principle on enlargement may not be easy to implement. Nevertheless, the priority accorded to enlarging the Union should concentrate minds on finding solutions to the institutional and policy differences among the existing member states. To those we now turn.

Political and institutional issues

Unlike the previous enlargement to the three EFTA countries, any future enlargement cannot take place under current institutional procedures. Fearing decision-making paralysis, the Corfu European Council of June 1994 stated that the 'institutional conditions for ensuring the proper functioning of the Union must be created at the 1996 IGC, which for that reason must take place before accession negotiations begin'.[17] This is mainly because the next enlargement will bring a decisive increase in the number of smaller and poorer states, altering the existing balance between large and small in ways that are likely to be unacceptable to the large states. Enlargement should therefore give a strong impetus not only to find solutions to already perceived problems, but to make them radical enough to cope with future needs in a wider EU. The Group of Reflection was concerned to ensure that enlargement should not 'weaken, change the nature of or actually break up the Union'.[18] Institutional reform 'is already necessary now, but the prospect of enlargement makes it imperative'.[19] From the long list of items, enlargement forces the IGC to consider in particular the Council's voting rules, the rotation of the Presidency, the size of the Commission, the appointment of Commissioners, and the representative capacity of the European Parliament in a Union of twenty and, later, thirty member states.[20]

The institutional issue presents itself most forcibly in the form of contention about voting powers in the key decision-making body, the Council, the circumstances in which majority voting will be deployed, the weights to be given to member states with different sizes of population, and the proportion of votes needed to form qualified majorities (and the inverse, the size of the blocking minority). So far the larger member states have been prepared to accept a system in which the smaller states have enjoyed a disproportionate share in the votes. Discontent with this system emerged on the accession of Austria, Finland and Sweden in 1995. That enlargement raised the number of Council votes from 76 to 87 (with the addition of 4 votes each for Austria and Sweden, and 3 for Finland), the (71%) qualified majority from 54 votes to 62, and the (29%) blocking minority from 22 to 26. The UK attempted, in a rather clumsy manner, to prevent the increase in the number of votes constituting a blocking minority. The 'Ioannina Compromise' of March 1994 resolved that where a vote produced a close result (a minority of between 23 to 25 votes), the Council 'will do all within its power to reach, within a reasonable time ... a satisfactory solution that can be adopted by at least 65 votes'.

This extraordinary arrangement — a type of institutionalised crisis management — works less than smoothly and leaves a bad odour in the present Union of fifteen member states. In a Union of, say, 27, with ten Central and East Europeans plus Cyprus and Malta, the total number of votes could increase to 138 with a blocking minority of 40. The share in total EU population of the four largest EU member states, Germany, France, the UK and Italy, would be reduced from 77% to 56%, but their share in Council votes would decline from 53% to only 30%. Since the newcomers would be mostly small and poor — with Poland large and poor — the voting weight of member states with a vested interest in receiving large net budgetary transfers would be increased substantially. Various suggestions as to how the question of voting weights could be resolved were discussed in our earlier Paper *Building the Union*, and there is no need to repeat the discussion here.[21] Our preferred solution would be a double majority system, requiring important decisions to be supported by states wielding two-thirds of the votes, but in addition containing two-thirds of the EU's total population. The Group of Reflection, for its part, gave no firm lead on this issue, and the Ioannina Compromise is set for a problematical re-negotiation at the IGC.

Rotation of the Council presidency every six months will face two serious problems in a much larger Union. First, each member state would have to wait a dozen or so years for its turn. Secondly, the capacity of two mini-states (Cyprus and Malta) and four very small states (Slovenia and the Baltics) to cope with the presidency would remain in doubt. The happy precedent of Luxembourg's many contributions as president cannot be assumed to apply. The Group of Reflection appeared to favour the idea of annual 'team presidencies' of, say, four member states.

The question of representation on the Commission has also arisen in the present EU of 15, with the growing perception that the present Commission of 20 members is unwieldy. Again, enlargement would exacerbate the problem and therefore intensifies the need to find a solution. Based on the present system, a scenario for seven states to join in the next round of enlargement would deliver up a Commission of 28 members. The problem can be resolved in a number of ways, also discussed in *Building the Union*, including reducing the number of Commissioners to one per member state; introducing a distinction between senior and junior Commissioners; or abandoning the system of national nominations and allowing an appointed — or, in the long run, even elected — President of the Commission to select a team on the basis of their political experience and expertise. On balance, we prefer the latter, radical solution.

Enlargement will require a restructuring of representation in the European Parliament. First, it would be impossible to expand the size of the Parliament simply by adding new MEPs on the existing basis. There is no alternative but to re-think how to provide parliamentary representation at EU level for up to 475 million citizens while keeping the Parliament at a manageable size. (The Group of Reflection suggests 700.) This may mean adjusting the system of degressive proportionality whereby the small states have privileged representation. But any new formula for the Parliament must be balanced against that of Council voting weights: in neither arm of the Union's legislature must the legitimate rights of the small states be overrun by the representatives of large ones. What is required for the Parliament is a genuinely uniform electoral procedure, as the Treaty indeed stipulates, based on proportional representation, within which a new gearing of MEPs per state population will be an important element.

Enlargement and security

The collapse of the Soviet system has destabilised Europe. The greatest danger would be posed by a resurgent, nationalist Russia. Central and East Europeans have reacted to the potential threat by expressing a strong if unfocused desire to conjoin with the Western system of collective security epitomised by Nato and the European Union.

The EU, for its part, has discovered a strong interest in building a Common Foreign and Security Policy (CFSP) that is effective throughout Europe, but especially on its eastern borders. The Union is also aware of the need to project its own security eastwards while simultaneously developing and maintaining good relations and close cooperation with Russia and the other CIS states. Likewise, the EU is rightly determined to retain the US guarantee of Europe's defence through Nato. But to extend the Union beyond Nato's existing scope without clarifying the contemporary meaning of Nato's security guarantee would make the EU highly vulnerable to entanglement in conflicts in Eastern Europe without having in place effective institutions and policies for handling them. This issue is particularly acute in the case of the Baltic States.

The US, supported by some EU governments, proposes that Nato should simply be extended eastwards to fill the security vacuum. Despite participating in the North Atlantic Consultative Council and Partnership for Peace organisations for maintaining good relations with Nato, Russia has regarded the extension of Nato membership as provocative.

In contrast with its attitude towards Nato expansion, Russia apparently has less objection to the extension of EU membership into Central Europe. Clearly, the EU as a civilian power has much to offer, having substantial diplomatic, economic and financial instruments with which to assist the reconstruction of Central and Eastern Europe. Rapid militarisation of the EU would be just as vexing to the Russians as the crude enlargement of Nato, if not more so. That is why we take a cautious approach to the first proposition and are hostile to the second.

In our previous Paper *Security of the Union* we suggested, first, that (Finland apart) the EU should not enlarge hurriedly up to the border of the Russian Federation; second, that Nato itself should not expand at this stage up to the borders of the old USSR; but that, third, the Nato security guarantee should be extended to embrace all the territory of the Union regardless of the commonalty of membership between the two organisations.[22]

This prescription for a balancing act is not just a concession to Russian sensibilities, but is also based on a critical assessment of the current capability of the European Union to secure its own external borders. Our proposals are expedient, but they do not pretend to be a permanent solution to pan-European security.

For one thing, they will work only so long as the USA remains fully committed to bearing the principal burden of Europe's defence. Nor will our arrangement maintain credibility if the EU fails to set in train and then to persevere with a comprehensive programme of measures to build up its own autonomous defence capability. This is envisaged by the Treaty of Maastricht, which speaks of 'the eventual framing of a common defence policy, which might in time lead to a common defence'.[23] Such a development is also postulated by the new partnership with the Western European Union, the military organisation within Nato involving only 10 of the current 15 member states of the EU.

The goal of enlarging the EU raises pointedly the question whether the member states can commit themselves to developing now a Common Foreign and Security Policy that is capable of operating after enlargement in the vulnerable area beyond its new eastern border. If they are not willing to do so, some member states may prefer not to widen the Union, so as to reduce the risks of involvement in disputes and even conflicts without the means or the will to take collective action to resolve them. But rejection of enlargement because the CFSP is too feeble to cater for it will not solve the problems of instability to the East. On the contrary, to shirk enlargement of the Union to those countries well-suited for accession would be an evasion of responsibility and would immediately exacerbate Europe's insecurity. Imagine how soon Greece could have got involved in the Balkans War had it not been a member of the European Union; and imagine how Turkey might have reacted had it been cast aside by Europe.

The EU cannot presume an indefinite and ever-ready US commitment to intervene in support of EU objectives, and, therefore, cannot hope credibly to project security into Eastern Europe in the longer term without improving the effectiveness of the CFSP, developing the WEU as the long-canvassed 'European Pillar' of Nato, and eventually merging the WEU into the EU and creating common defence forces to underpin an effective common foreign policy. Without such a determination, it would be dangerous to enlarge the Union eastwards.

To develop an effective CFSP for Eastern Europe would in no way be hostile to the US, nor would it mean abandoning close cooperation with the US in Nato for so long as the US is prepared to maintain its European presence. On the contrary, it would meet the many times reiterated wish of successive US administrations to see Europe sufficiently united to provide its own security. At present, however, discussions about the future of the EU on the one hand and of Nato on the other are curiously disjointed. For them to become fully coordinated, Nato should engage in an IGC process of its own. Parallel sessions of the two IGCs to discuss the security implications of EU enlargement could even be organised, and Central and East European states invited along to broaden and deepen the dialogue.

Progress, moreover, should now be made in the Balkans. After its initial disarray, and despite its frustration in the role of peacemaker, the European Union managed not to divide itself between the warring parties in ex-Yugoslavia as its member states would have done in former times. The Union is now in a strong position to offer a package of trade and aid agreements to the former combatants, with political strings attached. The EU must insist that the decisions reached in Dayton, Ohio are correctly applied, that refugees can return to their homes and that justice and the rule of law are resurrected. It should continually remind the Serbs, Croats and Bosnians that the European Union they might wish to join is a democratic edifice and that they will become welcome as members only if they apply human rights, protect minorities, end ethnic and religious discrimination, and establish properly functioning pluralist democracies.[24]

Internal threats to stability

Beyond the question of how to organise the security of an enlarged Union against external threats, lies the question of internal security. The accession of states in Central and Eastern Europe will accentuate the ethnic complexity and cultural diversity of the Union. Will it also raise insecurity?

The EU's single market establishes the principle of freedom of movement of people, not only to take up employment but to seek work, and to have their families join them. In the past, immigrants from poorer EU states such as Spain and Portugal, and from associated countries such as Turkey and Yugoslavia, were welcomed in the more industrial northern economies. Successive economic recessions, however, have increased unemployment with the result that cheap immigrant labour has been less welcome, and controls on immigration from outside the EU have been tightened. After 1989 the changes in eastern Europe aroused anxiety that millions of immigrant workers, refugees and asylum seekers might flood westwards into the Union.

Mass population movements have not come about on the scale that was feared in 1990, because people in Central and Eastern Europe have been much sturdier in coping with the pressures of transition than was expected; and conditions, although difficult, have not been as desperate as was anticipated. Moreover, the EU member states have increased the effectiveness of their immigration controls. Even so, the concentration of immigrants in Germany, France and Italy has provoked real social and racial tension. Germany's close partners, especially, must be sympathetic to its wish to see effective action taken at the IGC to strengthen cooperation in the field of justice and interior affairs. Urgent action is needed particularly to establish a common asylum policy; so also should the Dublin Convention on the crossing of external borders of the Union be brought into force as rapidly as possible.

We see no strong case, however, for attempting to restrict the free movement of persons throughout an enlarged Union, even on a transitional basis. For one thing, economic migration within the EU would stimulate the development of a more flexible labour market. For another, mass migration from the poorer, eastern half of the Union is hardly likely; the supply of low-skilled and low-paid jobs in the West is increasingly limited, and a mass exodus of younger and enterprising workers from new member states enjoying a higher rate of growth than the present EU is rather improbable. This leads us to consider the economic dynamics of an enlarged Union.

The economics of enlargement

There is a common assumption that enlarging the EU by admitting poor countries must impose burdens on the existing members. Therefore it is important to state that just as the original EC, and its successive enlargements, brought substantial benefits to the existing members, so the prospective enlargement to the East will bring substantial economic benefits, after taking into account any costs that will be incurred, to the EU in the early decades of the 21st century. The Central European economies are already growing faster than those in the EU. Being in the truest sense 'emerging economies', given access to EU markets and fair terms of accession they should continue for many years to grow faster than the more mature EU economies. Even though they take currently only a small proportion of total EU exports, the volume of exports from the present EU to Central and Eastern Europe has the potential to grow at annual average rates that have been estimated in excess of 10%.[25]

Such growth will increase the significance of Central and Eastern Europe in EU trade, and make a positive contribution to the growth of the EU economies. The applicant states will also contribute substantial gains to pan-European competitiveness, to be derived from combining the technology, capital and management skills of the West with the low-cost but highly skilled workers of the East.

Even more significant are the economic benefits of integration in terms of security — healing the post-war division of Europe, stabilising the politics of Central Europe, and embedding unified Germany more firmly in the centre of a wider EU. Although this prize is the basis of the EU's decision to widen the Union, the difficulty of quantifying the associated long-term financial benefit of peace and stability leads to it being ignored or minimised as politicians and officials focus on the budgetary costs of enlargement in the early years after accession. They would do well to consider how much less costly it would have been to support democratic and peaceful governments in former Yugoslavia before, rather than after, three years of internecine war and destruction.

The evidence for the long-term benefits of a wider Union is overlaid by a mutually contradictory catalogue of short-term economic and financial difficulties facing the EU as it contemplates enlargement:

- to admit the Central and East Europeans before they are ready would damage their emerging economies;
- jobs will be lost in the present Union because low wages will give the Easterners an unfair advantage in competition;
- given their low levels of GDP per capita, insupportable levels of financial transfers through agricultural policy and structural funds will be needed from the existing EU members;
- free movement of labour will mean massive flows of migrants into the EU if Central and Eastern Europe is allowed to accede before real income levels have risen much nearer to those in Western Europe.

How far are these real problems, and if so what solutions are available?

Trade relations and competitiveness

Imports from Central and Eastern Europe are only about 3% of total EU imports, but a more significant 15 - 20% of the one-fifth of EU trade conducted with non-OECD countries. These imports are growing fast. Exports from the Central and East European countries could increase by as much as 10 - 16% per annum as the full effects of trade liberalisation are felt.[26] According to the Commission, EU exports to Central and Eastern Europe grew by 22% in 1994, and imports by 27%. Not surprisingly the most rapid growth in EU imports from Central Europe has been in low technology goods or labour intensive products. The EU's export growth has been in high-tech and capital-intensive products.

Southern Europe faces more intense competition in its low-tech products, though it retains an advantage in the lighter, higher added-value items. The northern EU (here defined to include industrial northern Italy) stands to benefit from the increase in exports of high-tech, capital intensive products. But imports from the East compete with the products of unskilled labour in the northern EU and, assuming unchanged technology, could reduce the relative real wages of unskilled workers, with the effect concentrated in (northern) Italy and the UK. This comes at a time when there is already concern within the Union about the widening gap between the real wages of skilled and unskilled workers. Whether the potential effects continue as forecast on the basis of past trends depends on how successful industries are in adjusting to the shock of import competition. The key factor is industrial structure; both monopolised and fragmented industries tend to adjust slowly, industries with large firms but a competitive structure adjust more successfully. Overall, the adverse effects are thought to be small, and the gain to employment from improved global competitiveness of firms in the existing EU will compensate.

There is evidence from the textile, electronics, engineering and other sectors that firms in Western Europe benefit from 'outsourcing' — that is, organising part of their production process or component supply so as to take advantage of low unit labour costs in Central and Eastern Europe. Firms based inside the EU claim that they are able to retain their competitiveness with imports from Asia only by exploiting the opportunities for cost savings offered by this method. Such enterprise will be encouraged by trade liberalisation between the EU and the applicant states.[27]

The Europe Agreements

The Europe Agreements were signed in 1992 and 1993, and operated on an interim basis pending ratification in 1994. They offered the considerable advantage of a comprehensive framework for East-West Europe trade relations based on a commitment to free trade in industrial products. However, the Agreements continued to allow 'contingent' protection of EU markets through anti-dumping actions and safeguard measures (usually quotas) where imports were loosely defined as causing 'serious injury to domestic producers and bringing about serious deterioration in the economic situation of a region'. Even if these clauses were little used, the resulting uncertainty slowed down the process of restructuring and deterred investors, domestic and foreign. The dissatisfaction of Central and East European states with the operation of the Europe Agreements was shown in a number of tit-for-tat trade conflicts (for example, in the meat trade following an outbreak of foot-and-mouth disease).

At the Copenhagen European Council in June 1993 the EU approved a package of measures to liberalise the Europe Agreements. These included a reduction of the original six-year transition period for elimination of tariffs on imports of industrial goods except steel and textiles to three years: by the end of 1994 these goods entered the EU internal market free of duties; liberalisation of trade in sensitive products by speeding up the process of tariff elimination by one year, and augmentation of the quotas and ceilings on imports of sensitive goods by 20 to 25%.

Particularly important for Central and Eastern Europe is trade in so-called 'sensitive products'. Between 30% and 40% of their manufacturing employment was in the sensitive sectors at the beginning of the transition, and they represented 60% of EU imports.[28] The EU market offered substantial growth potential once the reform process got under way, and economic recession in Central Europe would certainly have been much worse without the rapid growth of exports to the EU.

The European Union adopted a similar approach to sensitive products in all its association agreements, as well as in transitional arrangements for new member states. Since the liberalisation process in Central Europe started at a time when the EU economies were both going into recession and facing intensified competition from dynamic Asian economies, the pressure to protect its sensitive sectors was particularly acute. By the end of 1995, however, with much structural adjustment already made, especially in the iron and steel industry, and the EU recovering from the recession, almost all constraints on exports from Central and Eastern Europe are supposed to have been removed, except for textiles.

In any event, the import surge was not been quite as anticipated in the 'sensitive' sectors, but in other categories, especially engineering and metal products, furniture and wood manufactures. The net effect of sensitive sector protection on EU employment is hard to quantify; the evidence suggests it was minimal or could even have been negative in that uncompetitive industrial structures were protected. In our view, restrictions on East-West trade, however motivated, are costly, since they tend to slow down the transition in the applicant states and distort markets in the EU.

Trade among the Central and East Europeans

The Central and East European states have also proved reluctant to liberalise trade among themselves, despite the negotiation of the Central European Free Trade Agreement made at Visegrad in 1992 (and joined by Slovenia in 1995). Trade cooperation is limited by historical antipathies, and particularly by the legacy of the discredited Council for Mutual Economic Assistance (Comecon) imposed by the Soviet Union. The newly independent and assertive governments of Central Europe fear, too, that the West wishes to consign their countries to a ghetto in which they are cut off from the benefits of integration with the EU. This hesitation is a pity, as a customs union could offer Central and Eastern Europe the significant benefits of increased volumes of trade and reduced dependence on bilateral trade with the Union. A customs union would help the applicant states to develop more complementary economic structures among themselves and to minimise frictions on accession to the EU.

An effective Central European common market would help to persuade foreign investors to view the region integrally, rather than as a set of fragmented markets. Setting up such an organisation would also provide an opportunity to renegotiate external trade relations, including the Europe Agreements, on a collective basis, and even to negotiate membership of the European Economic Area. Unfortunately, gaining in this way the advantages of effective inclusion in the single market is also interpreted by the Central and East Europeans (as it was by the members of EFTA) as confining them to an outer circle that does not meet their political needs. But the value of a proper customs union between the EU and the applicant states as the foundation of the pre-accession strategy makes sense.

Agriculture

In 1990 imports of agricultural produce from Central and Eastern Europe were subject to highly protective EU quota restrictions. High levels of protection were in part a reflection of political differences, and in part a justifiable response to economic distortions within the socialist command economies. The tariff reductions and increased quotas under the Europe Agreements were therefore significant.

European Union exports to Central Europe benefit from CAP export restitutions, defying normal expectations about comparative advantage. As reforms take effect in EU and Central European farming regimes, and as trade policies are modified, both sides should benefit from a trade in agricultural products which better reflects the underlying competitive advantages in different types of production and unit labour costs. Central Europe is much more rural than the present EU, with 25% of the workforce employed on the land as against only 6% in the West.[29] Achieving equilibrium between the two will be vital in order to secure the benefits from integrating East European farming into the CAP.

Much attention has been paid to the question of the size of the budgetary contributions from the EU's existing member states were the existing CAP to be applied across Europe. In addition to receipts from the CAP funds, both guarantee and guidance, the new member states would be entitled to substantial sums from the EU's structural funds. The net cost, after allowing for contributions from the new member states, has been estimated at 70% of the projected EU budget for 1999.[30] The Commission estimates much lower additional CAP expenditure of between Ecu 9 - 12 bn.[31] Estimates of this sort may be controversial, but they should succeed in concentrating minds on how to improve the competitiveness of European agriculture in general, and to cut subsidies.

So far little has been done except to signal the problems and list the theoretical solutions. But there has been real progress in curbing the worst excesses of the CAP through the MacSharry reforms coupled with those agreed in the context of the settlement of the Uruguay Round of GATT. The negotiations on the new ceiling for the EU budget that are to be conducted in parallel to the IGC will reveal the high politics of enlargement. In this perspective, the EU has no choice but to continue to decouple price support from food production, and to develop means of paying farmers for social and environmental activities. East European agriculture will have to be prepared for accession to the CAP by deep structural reform. This is another priority for the EU's pre-accession strategy.

The IGC has no remit to consider agricultural reform. However, if the EU is to confront the issues raised by enlargement, it should clarify urgently the strategic choices facing the Union on the extension of the CAP to Central and Eastern Europe. For their part, the applicant states would be wise to focus their attention on negotiating further access for their farm products to the EU market, rather than anticipating the benefits of subsidies from a CAP that is likely to be substantially altered before their accession.

Structural funds and the Union budget

When the socialist system collapsed in 1989 there were calls for an immediate 'Marshall Aid' programme of financial assistance to Eastern Europe, but this did not match the mood in the European Union. Some financial aid, as well as important technical assistance, has indeed been given, but there has been no massive, generous funding of the transformation process in Central and Eastern Europe. One of the clear benefits the applicant states may expect from EU membership, therefore, is large-scale financial assistance. Will they be disappointed?

The EU budget is only a tiny proportion, currently 1.20% (and programmed to rise only to 1.27% in 1998), of the aggregate GDP of the whole Union. But any increase in the total EU budget, and any change in the distribution among the member states of budgetary contributions and receipts, is highly controversial. According to one estimate, based on 1991 income levels, shares in agricultural production and existing EU agricultural and structural spending policies, the Central and East European states would receive substantial net transfers from the EU budget. The Commission's initial estimate that the structural funds will need to double in size should be taken seriously, despite the fact that the paucity of matching funds from inside the new member states will restrict their take-up.

Using these estimates and various assumptions about relative growth rates, it is possible to guess how many years would be needed before the Central and East European states could join the EU with neutral budgetary effects: that is, without receiving any net benefits from the EU budget, under present rules. The results are between 15 to 25 years.

This kind of cautious calculation is popular with governments that will have to obtain the consent of tax-paying voters to enlarging the Union. It is our view, however, that such an approach is misguided. Enlargement should not be pre-judged on the basis of budgetary calculations under existing EU policies, designed for a different EU in different circumstances. The level of transfers from richer to poorer member states in an enlarged EU will be decided by a complex balance of economic and political considerations, among which the effectiveness of aid to backward regions, and the degree of political solidarity within the Union, will be the most significant.

The belief that the scale of transfers will be comparable to those going from West to East within unified Germany is entirely misplaced. West Germans accepted, if with some reluctance, that their fellow countrymen were entitled to enjoy similar levels of real income. The European Union has never operated on this assumption, and will not do so now. Membership of the Union confers the opportunity, by competing in the single market and benefiting from economic and social cohesion, to increase prosperity, as both Italy, the poorest of the original Six, and Portugal, the poorest of the Twelve, have shown. The EU structural funds are to help the poorer states and regions adjust to competition in the wider market; they are recognition of the need for some redistribution of the economic gains from integration. They have never been, are not and will never be a social welfare system.

It is vital that the EU should adopt a realistic approach to the question of investing in the economic development of Central and Eastern Europe from which it has so much to gain in economic and political terms. Building the energy, transport and information technology infrastructures is a massive investment opportunity for western finance and a natural extension of the Trans-European Networks programme conceived at Maastricht and developed in the Delors 1993 White Paper, *Growth, Competitiveness, Employment.*[32] So also is the huge anti-pollution and conservation programme needed to make much of the former industrial complex created by Communism clean and safe.

This programme can be largely carried out not by governments on their own but by the operation of public-private partnerships that will unlock the huge potential of the integrated European capital market. Relatively small sums of public money can in the right circumstances lever out large sums of private sector finance, which will go to relieve the pressure on the EU's structural funds. However, there is a strong case for more than the EU's small technical assistance programmes so far available, supplemented by enhanced access to loans under concessional conditions from the European Investment Bank, the European Bank for Reconstruction and Development and other international agencies. The Phare programme could be adapted to become a more powerful financial instrument. Strategic public funding guided by the EU to projects inside the applicant states and linking them to the existing EU will only attract private investment of many times its size once the markets become confident that enlargement is politically assured, and that EU competition and regulatory frameworks will soon be made to apply. To this end, it would be helpful if the Union were soon to agree the parameters for the budgetary package that will be needed after 1998 to cope with enlargement. This will not be easy.

Enlargement and EMU

The Central and East European states will accede to an EU which is most likely to be operating a monetary union for a core group. An outer tier of member states will be made up of those who, either by accident or design, have not yet met the necessary convergence criteria. These states will have their exchange rates related to the single currency in some form of Exchange Rate Mechanism (ERM). This the new member states will probably be obliged to join until they, too, come to fulfil all the conditions for transition to the single currency, although the precise nature of the relationship between the EMU 'ins', 'pre-ins' and 'outs' is the subject of a current study by the Commission and the European Monetary Institute.

Some will argue that flexible exchange rates can, and in the absence of automatic fiscal stabilisers must, be used to allow the Central and East European economies to maintain competitiveness and full employment. This argument is based on false assumptions. Failure to control inflation in the domestic economy would surely make exchange rate adjustments inevitable, but this would imply a failure of macro-economic stabilisation and/or of micro-economic restructuring. Each devaluation of a Central and East European currency would damage its credibility and reduce the attraction of the region as a suitable location for overseas investment.

Freedom of capital movements, established in the EU by 1990, and which facilitated the exponential growth of capital movements, has been shown in the European monetary crises of the last few years to be essentially incompatible with adjustable exchange rates, and floating exchange rates have been found to be inconsistent with the single market. If the new member states were exempted during a transitional period from freedom of movement of capital, they would lose the benefits of full participation in the integrated European capital markets vital for their economic growth. Independent exchange rate policies are needed now during their transition to the market economy. But once the transformation has been achieved, there will be no acceptable alternative in the long term to the adoption of flexible wage policies and concentration on improving the supply side of the economy. The convergence criteria for joining EMU make eminent sense for the Central and Eastern economies as they seek to catch up with the rest of the EU. The Maastricht conditions are in fact remarkably similar to the targets Central and East European governments are setting for the good management of their own economies. Moreover, although they have had difficulty in bringing inflation under control, the performance of some of the applicant states, such as the Czech Republic, has not been notably worse than that of several EU member states.

A Union for the whole of Europe

At the European Council in Essen in December 1994, a structured pre-accession strategy was laid out, involving the phased adoption by the applicant countries of the acquis communautaire. Cooperation would develop in a whole range of flanking policies. Ministers and parliamentarians from the applicant states are to develop a regular pattern of meetings with the EU institutions. At the heart of the preparation for accession is adaptation to the Union's single market regime, with the promise of increasing levels of trade once basic disciplines are in place. Agriculture is also considered to be a key element of the strategy. The Essen package is a 'route plan for the associated countries as they prepare for accession', and adds up to an ambitious pre-accession transitional period.[33]

The Madrid European Council one year later continued this approach. The leaders reiterated their previous statement that the applicant countries would be treated on an equal basis, and called on the Commission to prepare a composite report on all aspects of enlargement as well as its opinions on individual applications as soon as possible after the conclusion of the IGC. It also asked the Commission to produce a report on the revision of the Union's financing system immediately after the end of the IGC. With regard to the IGC itself, the European Council promised consultations with representatives from applicant states on a two-monthly basis. This approach is to be welcomed.

The conditions for the applicants are tough, and, although some increase in Phare expenditure is forseen, the European Union is simultaneously reducing the financial benefits of membership. The formal association agreements and the Essen package grants only limited participation by the applicants in EU decision-making; the implication is that full accession and enjoyment of the comprehensive benefits of membership will be delayed until there is evidence of real economic convergence and until EU reforms have sufficiently reduced the costs of enlargement to the existing members.

An alternative, and more drastic, proposal for a form of limited membership could be devised. In deference to the political imperatives for ending the isolation of the former Communist countries, membership of some second (or even third) tier of the EU could be negotiated. Certain applicants could be offered a partial membership of the EU that excluded them from the CAP, the structural funds and free movement for workers, with only limited access to other decision-making; or they could be offered phased-in membership of other policy areas based on clearly stated criteria being met. But as we have noted above, such an arrangement would be similar to the European Economic Area, and it would be bound to be unpalatable to the applicants from Central and Eastern Europe who are attracted to full membership of the Union because of its potential contribution to domestic stability, economic prosperity and international security.

More realistic is to narrow the gap between the aspirations of Central and Eastern Europe and the realities of European Union membership by combining rigorous reform of EU policies — ideally, with special emphasis on measures to combat unemployment — with well-programmed preparatory and transitional periods. The precedent of Portugal, which had a pre-accession structural adjustment programme, is encouraging in this respect. What the Union governments cannot at present agree upon, unfortunately, is the essential third element in the enlargement formula: the reinforcement of the common institutions so that they will be able to cope efficiently and effectively with the job of running a much larger Union.

Political leadership of a high quality is essential if enlargement of the Union is to be accomplished on a time-scale and on terms acceptable to both sides. Such leadership is available from Germany, but must now be matched in other member states if the IGC is to have a successful outcome and is not to dash the hopes of the Union's neighbours to the East and to the South. Present evidence gives few grounds for optimism that those who care passionately about the future of Europe will not be disappointed by the IGC.

It would be unworthy of a British government to hamper the unification of eastern and western Europe. Yet this would be the result if the UK were to refuse at the IGC to deepen the European Union. Continued resistance to institutional reform will at the very least delay the widening of the Union or, worse, stop it altogether. Conversely, the more radical the reform of EU policies and institutions the sooner enlargement can take place and the shorter the transition periods can be.

The IGC of 1996 is a golden opportunity to broker a package deal designed to make the Union work for the whole of Europe. The essential element is that the UK should concede institutional reform in return for French and German concessions on policy. The main institutional priorities are more majority voting in the Council; co-decision and electoral reform for the Parliament; some degree of communitarisation of justice and home affairs, including wider jurisdiction for the Court of Justice. In policy terms, a restructuring of the CAP and the structural funds is paramount; and a more positive attitude to developing the Union's common foreign and security policy alongside Nato is the other major priority.

What is needed at this stage is firm agreement between all parties that enlargement has to take place but that it must be accompanied by the necessary policy, financial and institutional reforms.

The history of the EU is littered with half measures. On this occasion, to make a Union for the whole of Europe, half-measures may not be enough. We agree strongly with the IGC's Group of Reflection, which in its final report to the leaders, insisted that enlargement 'provides a great opportunity for the political reunification of Europe'.

> 'Not only is it a political imperative for us, but it represents the best option for the stability of the continent and for the economic advancement not just of the applicant countries but for this Europe of ours as a whole. That enlargement is not an easy exercise. Its impact upon the development of the Union's policies will have to be assessed. It will require efforts both by applicants and present Union members that will have to be equitably shared. It is therefore not only a great chance for Europe but also a challenge. We must do it, but we have to do it well.'[34]

NOTES

[1] Geoffrey Denton, Senior Research Fellow at the Federal Trust, contributed the basic draft of this Paper.

[2] For a discussion of the strategic setting of the IGC, see Federal Trust Papers No. 1, *State of the Union*, London, Federal Trust, February 1995.

[3] EC *Bulletin*, No. 6, June 1993, p. 13.

[4] For an early statement of the political values of the Community, see the *Declaration on democracy* made by the European Council in Copenhagen in April 1978; EC *Bulletin*, No. 3, 1978, pp. 5-6.

[5] Statistical Office of the European Communities, *Eurostat Reviews 1973 - 1982, 1977 - 1986* and European Commission, *Interim Report to the European Council on the effects on the policies of the EU of enlargement to the associated countries of Central and Eastern Europe*, Brussels, December 1995.

[6] GDP per capita at market exchange rates are available for 1994, but are not used as nominal exchange rates introduce distortions and grossly underestimate the GDPs expressed in dollars. The percentages are calculated from the 1993 estimates of GNP per capita at purchasing power parity (PPP) exchange rates, published in the European Bank for Reconstruction and Development *Transition Report*, November 1995. But the use of PPP rates is itself controversial. They do not solve the problem of measuring the contribution of the 'grey' economy, and therefore probably substantially underestimate the GDP of the Central and Eastern European economies.

[7] Article O of the Treaty on European Union.

[8] European Commission, *Eurobarometer*, Brussels, 42, Spring 1995, p. 50.

[9] Ernst & Young, *Central and Eastern Europe — Winners and Losers: A Study of the Practical Implications of Further European Integration*, London, 1995.

[10] *Eurobarometer*, op. cit., p. 49. See also Richard Rose and Christian Haerpfer, 'Democracy and Enlarging the European Union Eastwards', in *Journal of Common Market Studies*, Vol. 33, No. 3, 1995.

[11] Comparisons of GDP per capita using market exchange rates show Romania with 41% of the EU average in 1994, above Hungary. But calculations on the EBRD's PPP basis reduce this to under 20%, according to the Economist Intelligence Unit (*The Economist*, 9 December 1995).

[12] See also *State of the Union*, op. cit, p.17.

[13] EC *Bulletin*, Supplement, No. 5, 1993, p. 17.

[14] For the conclusions of the Madrid summit, see the discussion on p. 37 below.

[15] See *Reflection Group's Report*, Brussels, 5 December 1995, p. 9.

[16] *Agence Europe*, 9 December 1995.

[17] EC *Bulletin*, No. 6, 1994, p. 14.

[18] *Reflection Group's Report*, op. cit., p. 3.

[19] *Reflection Group's Report*, op. cit., p. 23.

[20] We will discuss the related question of the size and appointment of the Court of Justice in our forthcoming Federal Trust Papers No. 6, *Justice and Fair Play*.

[21] For a more detailed discussion, see Federal Trust Papers No. 3, *Building the Union: reform of the institutions*, London, Federal Trust, July 1995.

[22] For a fuller discussion of these issues, see Federal Trust Papers No. 4, *Security of the Union*, London, Federal Trust, November 1995.

[23] Article J.4.1.

[24] See Boris Vukobrat, *The Chairman's Letter*, Paris la Défense, Peace and Crises Management Foundation, No. 55, 1995.

[25] Riccardo Faini and Richard Portes (eds), *European Trade with Eastern Europe*, London, Centre for Economic Policy Research, 1995, pp. 93-94.

[26] Richard E. Baldwin, *Towards an Integrated Europe*, London, Centre for Economic Policy Research, 1994, p. 101.

[27] For example, an account of ABB's investment in the 13 countries of Central and Eastern Europe: 'ABB secures lower cost sources of components such as turbines and switch-gear ... up to 40% cheaper than Western suppliers ... which helps to win international market share against tough competition'; *Financial Times*, 10 January 1996. See also Kevin Done, 'The growing trend towards the East', *Financial Times*, 19 January 1996.

[28] J. Rollo and A. Smith, 'The political economy of Eastern European trade with the European Community: why so sensitive?', *Economic Policy*, April 1993.

[29] See the European Commission, *The Agricultural Strategy Paper* (Fischler Report), Brussels, December 1995.

[30] Baldwin, op. cit, p. 176.

[31] Fischler Report, op. cit.

[32] For three Federal Trust reports on the financing and management of such a recovery programme, see *The Pension Time Bomb in Europe* and *Network Europe and the Information Society*, both London, Federal Trust, 1995, and *Private Enterprise and Public Utility in the European Union*, forthcoming.

[33] See EC *Bulletin*, No.12, 1994, pp. 20-26.

[34] *Reflection Group's Report*, op. cit., p. ii.